The SECRET LANGUAGE
TO IMPROVE YOUR

FOR PERSONAL SUCCESS
STAYING POSITIVE
AND HAPPY

ROBERT TODD

The Secret Language
To Improve Your Life For Personal Success Staying Positive And Happy

Copyright © 2021 by Robert Todd.

Paperback ISBN: 978-1-63812-142-8
Hardcover ISBN: 978-1-63812-172-5
Ebook ISBN: 978-1-63812-143-5

All rights reserved. No part in this book may be produced and transmitted in any form or by any means, electronic, or mechanical, including photocopying, recording, or by any information storage and retrieval system, without permission in writing from the copyright owner.

The views expressed in this work are solely those of the author and do not necessarily reflect the views of the publisher hereby disclaims any responsibility for them.

Published by Pen Culture Solutions   10/23/2021

Pen Culture Solutions
1-888-727-7204 (USA)
1-800-950-458 (Australia)
support@penculturesolutions.com

Acknowledgements

I would like to thank everyone who has assisted me in the preparation of this book and in particular thank my wife Judy for her help and support.

Contents

About the Author viii
Introduction xi
The Search 1
The Approach 6
Lesson One 8
Rivers Of Reaction 12
Positive Thesaurus 17
Combined Negatives 21
Triggers To Remember 25
Double Negatives 27
Positive Environments 31
The Laws Of Positive Language 33
The Laws Of Positive Language 35
Law 1 37
Words Have Power 39
Pygmalion 43
Self And Positive Language 48
Children And Positive Language 57
Law 2 66
Proverbs And Truisms 68
Law 3 74
Health 79
Self Talk 86
Law 4 90
Imagination And Belief 92

Praise Phrases 98
Law 5 101
Affirmations 104
Using Affirmations 112
Law 6 114
Words Create Our Future 116
We Choose The Words We Use 120
Steps To Positive Language 129
Quotations From This Book 134
Listing 139

About the Author

Robert Todd ran his own training company in negotiations, interpersonal skills, relaxation, meditation and communications, was a motivational speaker throughout Australia and New Zealand for twenty three years. He has also helped hundreds of people as a clinical hypnotherapist and counsellor.

This Is The Story Of Thomas And Peter As Told By Thomas.

THOMAS IS UNSURE AND DOUBTING.

PETER IS POSITIVE AND CARING.

THOMAS AND PETER REPRESENT MYSELF AND MANY OF THE THOUSANDS OF WONDERFUL MEN AND WOMEN I HAVE WORKED WITH.

SOMETIMES PEOPLE ACT LIKE THOMAS, SOMETIMES LIKE PETER.

IT'S THE PETER IN YOU THAT CREATES YOUR SUCCESS AND CONTENTMENT.

THIS BOOK IS ABOUT USING YOUR PETER TALENTS MORE, AND LAYING THE FOUNDATION FOR SUCCESS AND CONTENTMENT.

* * * * * * *

Introduction

The Secret Language presents you with a new approach to achieving success.
It is based on years of experience in advising, training, observing and listening to people in action in many of Australia's top companies. The result, almost 20 years of information, has been distilled into this volume which explains how people removed the barriers that had been preventing them from succeeding.

The Secret Language is for all those positive people who want to reach their full potential.

The Secret Language will unlock the enormous potential people have, for creating and enjoying a life of success and fulfilment.

We encourage you to continue listening to teachers, reading about and putting into practice positive philosophies, and to have faith that the power within you can be directed to achieving wonderful things in your life.

When you put into practice what you learn about the power of positive language, you will achieve all you want, with greater ease.

Robert Todd

The Search

It's amazing how well I feel these days. My body seems lighter, yet my weight is the same. It's as though I am a free spirit, apart from my physical self. Things are going well for me and I smile when I think back to the times when they weren't.

I'd realised as a young man that the power of positive thinking resulting in a Positive Mental Attitude (PMA) was the medium by which I could take control of my life and achieve everything I wanted.

Successful people around the world testified to the power of being positive in their personal and business life.

As a young man, I had purchased a copy of Napoleon Hill's "Laws of Success". Napoleon Hill convinced me that successful business people use PMA. Successful parents and students use PMA. Successful professional people, doctors, scientists, sports people and others use PMA.

I knew that if I were to be successful, I must be positive, and ***there are no shortcuts to success.***

So I ventured into the world of business. I worked for major companies in minor jobs. Eventually, after some **difficulty**, I gained executive positions and felt that PMA was working.

I began to build up an extensive library of books and tapes on PMA. "***If I'm ever going to make it*** to the top, I will first have to master this art of being positive" I thought.

I started my own business and was exhilarated when my first sales came, and then more followed.

"It's amazing what you can do when you think positively" I thought.

However, lean times came and sales faltered. I was downcast, felt dejected and rejected. We had a major robbery, our under-insured factory burned down, and my business failed. It seemed ***bad luck comes in threes.***

"***If at first you don't succeed, then try, try again***" my spirit said. "Doesn't PMA tell you that ***failure is but opportunity in disguise?***"

So I determined to ***try*** again, and this time I would follow the principles of positive thinking to the letter.

My goal plan had been determined, both short and long term. My research was extensive. I knew where I was going, and was determined to get there in my personal and business life.

It hadn't become any easier since the last time I'd ***tried***. It was as if ***I wanted to succeed, but the rest of the world didn't want it.***

"Positive thinking is all very well" I thought, "***but*** *it isn't easy.*"

However, by keeping to my positive approach, the business grew and I was soon employing 12 people. *I hoped* all would keep going well.

With an increased staff came increased *problems*. Then again, I believed *something that comes easily is not worth having*. Our sales were growing, *but* our costs were growing as well.

"*Win some - lose some*" I thought. "*If only* all my employees shared my enthusiasm for positive thinking". I *tried* regularly to convince them.

Then, to make matters worse, an economic recession set in. It all seemed *impossible*. Selling my product became increasingly complicated because of the uncertainties of the market.

Fortunately the recession was only temporary, *but* it shook me and my business considerably.

As I closed the office one evening, I sighed "*I wish* things could be easier. I can be a success and I know it. I can see it. Everything is in place. Why can't my business take off? Why is it plodding along instead of running? Have I reached the limit of my ability? Am I not doing it correctly?"

I became determined to find the answer to my dilemma, and to establish an environment in my company which would positively harness the strength of everyone working in it. *But* would I be able to do it?

If only I could find the answer to this question, then *I ought to be able* to inspire everybody working in my organisation to be more positive.

I thought "If I were ill, I'd visit a doctor. If my machinery broke down, I would call a technician. ***But what do I do*** if my positive thinking isn't working? Maybe ***two heads are better than one***."

From time to time I had attended seminars where visiting trainers from overseas were quite inspirational, ***but*** I wanted to discuss personally with a successful exponent, the practical application of being positive, and not the theoretical concept.

Discussing this with a friend, who is a very successful businessman, he suggested I call Peter.

Peter is something of a guru in the field of managerial thinking. He is an extremely positive person, very much into whole-brain thinking and mind management. My friend had attended a stimulating training session conducted by Peter a few months earlier, and apparently his "laid back" easy-to-listen-to advice on mind management had left a deep and lasting impression.

I realised Peter was a successful business executive, trainer and Keynote Speaker. ***If only*** I could persuade him to see me personally, ***maybe*** he could help with my dilemma.

* * * * * * *

There Are Two Kinds

Of Knowledge,

Knowledge We Know

And

Knowledge

We Can Find.

Robert Todd

The Approach

Peter remembered my friend when I telephoned, and said "Yes, I will be very happy to talk with you. From what you've said so far, I feel I have the answer for you."

This sounded encouraging, ***but*** was it ***too good to be true***?

"You've met people with similar ***problems*** to mine before, then?" I asked.

"Yes, I have, many times. You sound ready to listen and learn, in which case I'm happy to see you."

"Well, he certainly comes across positively" I thought, as I hung up the phone and prepared for the meeting we had planned.

* * * * * * *

The Individual's

Whole Experience

Is Built

Upon The Plans

Of His Language .

Henri Delacroix

Lesson One

Peter rose from his chair to meet me. A tall man with a relaxed manner, well groomed, he greeted me warmly.

We discussed my friend and the course he had attended. Peter told me it was his latest programme which dealt in detail with the language of the mind.

We relaxed in armchairs and I began to tell him of my *problem*. "*I try to succeed, but it seems as if the world doesn't want it.*"

"Well, Thomas, from what you've told me, I'd say it's a situation where the spirit is willing and the words are weak."

"What do you mean 'From what I've told you'? I've said only a few words."

Peter laughed. "Can you remember the words you used?" he asked.

"I said something like "I try to succeed, but it seems as if the world doesn't want me to."

"Exactly. You've triggered two Rivers of Reaction which are working against your plan to be positive."

"You mean I've studied PMA for years, attended training courses, listened to tapes in the car, read dozens of books, even given PMA talks to my kids; and after uttering one sentence, you tell me I'm working against my own plan to be positive?"

"Oh, your situation sounds reasonable to me. From what you told me on the phone, I know you would like your business to be more successful. It is solvent. You've held some responsible positions with major companies. You have a happy family and good friends. You are success-ful."

"Yes. *I guess I am successful, but ... ...*"

"There you go again" Peter said with a smile.

"What do you mean 'There I go again'?"

"Before I explain the Rivers of Reaction, tell me exactly why you're here today."

"Well, *I'm hoping to try and find out* why I'm not achieving the goals I set for myself, even though I know *I should be achieving them. I think* my goals are reasonable and within my ability. I also want to know *if it's possible* to have everyone who works for my company thinking positively."

Peter settled back in his chair and considered my request.

"Your perseverance and determination will make it work for you, when you combine these with PL."

"PL?"

"Positive Language.

You see, the people who succeed, the people who get what they want in life - whether it be wealth, material possessions, deep friendships or peace of mind - do so because they speak a special language."

"A special language?" I said. "How do I learn this special language?"

"Oh, it's not like learning ancient Greek or Latin; in fact, you already know all the words that will bring you the success you want. The secret lies in choosing which words to use and the combinations you make of them."

"Do you mean" I ventured "saying things positively rather than tentatively?"

"That's part of it. You hear people say *'Maybe, there's a possibility that, if we tried, we might be successful'* rather than 'This is a good idea. Let's make a success of it'."

It's true, I thought, that the successful people I know speak very confidently. I'd always thought they spoke confidently because they were successful, but maybe they are successful because they speak confidently.

I put this idea to Peter.

"Definitely" he said. "The way people speak and the words they use, steer them and propel them towards success.

The English language is so wonderfully rich in shades of meaning and expression. It gives us the opportunity to express ourselves powerfully.

This opportunity is often lost because we choose the wrong words, or use the wrong combination of words. Without thinking, we use phrases, such as *'win some, lose some'* or *'bad luck comes in threes'* or maybe *'too good to be true'*. These statements work against us."

I listened carefully, and thought "These are typical statements I make. I'm going to learn a lot today ... ..."

* * * * * *

Rivers Of Reaction

"Would you please explain your comments on my first words to you when we met today?"

"Certainly. You said '*I try to succeed, but it seems as if the world doesn't want it*'.

When you said that, you set in motion two Rivers of Reaction in your mind.

The first River was triggered by the word '*try*' in 'I try to think positively.' The word '*try*' usually means we are not expecting to succeed.

In our mind's Experiences File, there are hundreds of examples of the times we '*tried*' to do things and failed, so a reaction of '*I'll try*' means 'I feel uncertain about the idea of succeeding'."

"Is this what you mean?" I asked. "Only last Saturday, I was at a sports carnival and I heard a mother say to her son '*Try to win, but don't get your hopes up, or you'll be too disappointed if you lose*.'

Is that the sort of thing you have in mind?"

"Yes. Because *'try'* is sometimes used to apologise, or prepare us for failure in advance."

"Can that be true, Peter?

It seems to me that the intention is the important thing. Some people will say *'try'*, and to them it means *to do their very best*."

"That's true, if this is what the child believes. In that case, it would be better for their parent to say 'Do your best to win' because it would stimulate a River of Reaction towards possible success.

I believe the easiest way to explain the Rivers Of Reaction is with an example.

Imagine that you are lost in a forest. As darkness falls and it starts to get cool, you follow a little-used path.

It is the traditional dark and stormy night. You come upon an old, deserted, one room hut, and take shelter as it begins to rain.

The room is bare and for warmth, you huddle in a corner, pull your coat collar up around your ears, and settle down to sleep.

You're awakened by a noise - a screechy, dragging sort of noise.

You immediately sit bolt upright, eyes popping. Your mind starts moving at a great speed."

"Your Rivers of Reaction are flowing rapidly. The conscious part of your mind asks 'What's that?'

Your subconscious speedily sorts through it's Experiences File and says … …

'It could be an intruder ... ... Or the wind moving something ... ... Or a wild animal ... ... Or rats ... ... Or ... ... a ghost !!'

Your heart beat increases.

Just as quickly, your subconscious mind triggers possible reactions ... ...

'Stay still and listen ... ... Pretend it's not there ... ... Search for a weapon ... ... Get up and investigate ... ...'

The subconscious flashes these possibilities to your conscious mind.

Your logical conscious mind considers the possible reactions. It decides to listen and observe intensely.

Then you notice there is a broken window that is being buffeted by the wind .. ... you realise this is the noise, and it's O.K.

You calm down and relax."

"A similar thing happens every time you have an experience, whether it's real or imagined. When-ever you see, feel or hear something, your mind records and files your reaction. That reaction will be recalled the next time a similar situation occurs, and your response will be based on a review of those reactions.

This mental process of questioning, evaluating, deciding and reacting, is going on all the time; and we call this your 'Rivers of Reaction'.

A similar reaction applies every time you say or hear a word: it sets off a River of Reaction.

Some words stimulate a positive reaction, while others create a negative response.

This is why it is important to avoid words that can create a negative response, like *'try'*.

Let's look at another word, the word *'but'*. How many times have people said to us *'That's a good idea but... ...'* or *'What you're saying is O.K. but... ...'*

As soon as we hear the word *'but'* we know what follows is going to be a downer, a negative statement. It's as though the words that come before the *'but'* are ignored; they are overshadowed by what follows."

"I see what you mean about *'try'* or *'but'*. What other words create negative reactions?"

"Take the word *'should'*. How many times do you say *'I should clear up my desk'* and how often does it get done?

Or you might say 'The Atkins Company is our biggest client. We *'should'* contact them every week'. The word *'should'* means we will probably put it off. Or, it means we have to do something when nobody really wants to.

Even the word *'problem'* stimulates a defeatist attitude in some people's minds. A *'problem'* causes them to worry, therefore it activates a negative River of Reaction. I suggest, instead, we say 'situation' or 'event'."

* * * * * * *

Men Imagine That

Their Minds

Have Command Of

Language

Yet Language

Bears Rule

Over Their Mind .

Francis Bacon

Positive Thesaurus

"**I** believe you want a new way of expressing yourself, which involves eliminating negative words from your language, and selecting from a *'Positive Thesaurus'*.

The idea is for you to consciously think of, and use, positive words, so you can produce positive reactions in yourself and others. It requires discipline to recognise and discard the words that have negative connotations, and stimulate a negative impact."

"I guess that words can be either positive, negative or neutral" I said "and we must use positive ones wherever possible?"

"Thomas, it's important to remember that it's the connotation of the word that we must recognise, and many people fail to realise that certain words have a negative connotation.

As well as *'try'*, *'but'* and *'should'*, which are negative, there are many other words we use in everyday conversation that continually create negative reactions in ourselves and others."

"What are some of the negative words you have noticed me using?"

"Here's a list of words I believe you want to avoid, their apparent meaning, and some substitutes you may like to use:

NEGATIVE INDICATOR	SUBSTITUTE
Try (Do not expect to succeed)	Will, Test, Plan Experiment.
But (Switches person to negative section of mind)	And, Then.
Should (Agree and don't intend to, or don't want to)	Could, Will, Want to.
Wish or Hope (Things we want, and do not expect to get)	Want.

NEGATIVE INDICATOR	ACTION
Ought (When substituted for 'should')	(Delete)

NEGATIVE INDICATOR	ACTION
If only (Refusal to accept event)	(Delete)

However
    (When substituted
    for the word 'but')
	(Delete)

Impossible (When used as an excuse)	(Delete)
Difficult (Creates barriers)	(Delete)
Problem (Creates barriers)	(Delete)
Just (Meaning 'merely')	(Delete)

Only
    (When used in a
    depreciative way)
	(Delete)

"As I reviewed the list, and reflected with unease upon how often I used words such as these, I asked Is it only words, or phrases too?"

* * * * * *

Change Our Words,

Change Our Way Of Speaking,

Change Our Way Of Thinking,

Then We Can Change

Other Aspects

Of Our Life .

Robert Todd

Combined Negatives

"Yes, it's phrases as well. Let's look at combined negatives. Here's a test. I want you to do exactly as I say. O.K?"

"O.K." I said.

"Don't think of an orange."

Of course, the first thing I thought of was an orange.

"This is because the word *'don't'* is a non-visual word" Peter continued "and therefore is missed by the subconscious. The remainder of the sentence 'think of an orange' creates an image at the conscious level.

Here is how that applies to life.

A husband may be visiting his wife in hospital and she asks him how everything is going at home. He replies *'Don't worry.'*

The word *'don't'* is ignored, and the word *'worry'* stimulates a River of Reaction which immediately reminds the wife of several things that could have gone wrong, and she starts to worry."

"I suppose the person who said *'Don't worry'* would be more positive if their words were 'Everything is OK?'"

"Yes, it would have a more positive effect.

The point I want to make is, that the effect produced on other people by talking to them negatively, with words such as *'don't'*, can promote the very thing we want to avoid.

Let me give you a few more examples.

You often hear people say *'don't forget'*.

When this happens, our subconscious mind recognises only the word *'forget'*. Unless we make a conscious effort to over-ride it, our subconscious will trigger the reaction to forget."

Then Peter showed me another example, a letter he had received from a person working with a very large company. The writer was concerned with the increased amount of accidents at work.

Their injury rate, since a recent safety logo was introduced, was the worst for a decade. The writer wondered if the new safety campaign logo could be a contributing factor. .Peter recommended a new logo and injuries went down lower than ever before.

This was the logo: This was the new logo

In the first logo, the mind only registers the word

'INJURIES' in second *'**SAFETY**'*

THE SUBCONSCIOUS IGNORES
NON-VISUAL WORDS,
AND TREATS IMAGES AS POSITIVE.

As I listened, I thought of the many times I had said to my staff "*Don't forget to phone* so and so" or "*Don't leave the machine running*", and then felt frustrated and angry when they forgot to phone or left the machine running. Of course, I can see now that it was me who created the situation.

"So, combined negatives are to be avoided?" I asked.

"Yes" replied Peter. "When you eliminate combined negatives, such as *'don't worry'* and *'don't forget'*, you will increase your accomplishments and your positive feelings towards life.

Let's make a list of them, with possible alternatives:

    DON'T WORRY - EVERYTHING IS O.K.

    DON'T FORGET - REMEMBER

    DON'T BE LATE - BE ON TIME

    DON'T SPEED - DRIVE WITHIN THE LIMITS

    NOT WRONG - RIGHT

    NOT DIFFICULT - EASY

    NO WORRIES - O.K.

    NO PROBLEMS - O.K."

I wondered if there were any special techniques to have people remember. I put this question to Peter.

****

Triggers To Remember

"There is a special way to have people remember an instruction. How you express something is as important as the words you choose, when using positive language" Peter said.

"When we say 'Joe, remember tomorrow to bring the Johnson plans', what could happen is that tomorrow, when Joe arrives at the office, the first thing he remembers is the Johnson plans - and they're still at home.

If you had used a trigger such as *'when you arrive home tonight*, Joe, remember to get the Johnson plans to bring to the office tomorrow', when Joe *arrived home*, he would remember the plans and placed them ready to take to work."

"I can see what you mean" I mused. "The idea is to have the person prompted with a trigger where it is wantded?"

"Yes. For example, an apprentice is being trained to assemble a machine. A good trainer will use a trigger such as *'When you pick up the return valves*, remember to insert the seals'. If the trainer had said 'Remember to put in the seals', there is no trigger, and a good chance the apprentice will remember after the machine has been assembled."

"I understand. We want to place a trigger in a person's mind when we give instructions.

'When you arrive home tonight' was a trigger for Joe, and 'when you pick up the return valves' was the trigger for the apprentice?"

"Yes, the idea is to mentally picture the person doing what we want them to do, when we want them to do it, and by our words we transfer that picture, with the trigger, to their mind."

"That is a good way to have people remember instructions, Peter.

Are there any other hints, or changes I want to make?"

* * * * * *

Double Negatives

"Some people use double negatives when they think they are expressing themselves positively.

When they give a compliment, they say '*They're not an unattractive person*' or when answering a question, they say '*You're not wrong*'.

When you hear such statements phrased in the negative, they are less powerful than positive words."

"That's true, Peter. I often hear the expression 'You're not wrong' which seems to be a waste of words, as well as having negative connotations."

"Yes, that's a popular one these days.

Here's another example.

Say '*We can't fail*' several times out loud; then say 'We will win'. You'll notice a difference in your reaction.

Our mind misses the '*can't*' and reacts to the '*fail*'.

By having a negative word at the end of the sentence, we draw attention to it; therefore it is better to finish with a positive word."

"You mean, instead of saying '*That's not a bad idea*', '*You're not wrong*' and '*We can't fail*', in future I will say 'That's a good idea', 'You're right' and 'We will win'?"

"Yes, that's it. Interesting that these simple changes have an effect on you? You will have a more positive feeling towards yourself, others, and life in general."

* * * * * * *

Change Your Language

And You Change

Your Thoughts

Robert Todd

Change Your Thoughts

And You Change

Your World.

Norman Vincent Peale

Positive Environments

"**B**y using positive language, we can create a positive environment in which only phrases with positive connotations are used.

Therefore, looking at your family situation, and thinking back to the word *'can't'* together with the word *'problem'*, you will find that statements such as *'I can't solve the problem'* are translated into positives such as 'I want your help with this situation'.

This way, you can delete *'can't'* and *'problem'* from your family vocabulary.

PL is used to create a positive, environment in the home which is a benefit to every member of your family and creates harmony."

I wondered "Is it really possible or practical to use positive words only … … ?"

* * * * * * *

When You Understand

The Laws Of Positive Language,

When You Use

Positive Language,

When You Experience

The Power Of Positive Language,

You Can Have

Positivity Working For You.

Robert Todd

The Laws Of Positive Language

"It is possible and it is practical to avoid words with negative connotations, and to use positive words" Peter replied.

"There are other areas we want to discuss, and the best way to explain is to start with the Laws of Positive Language.

When you understand these Laws, you will see how using positive language can unlock a powerful tool which is available to us all."

"Laws of Positive Language?" I asked.

"Yes, there are six Laws of Positive Language that affect everything in our lives; our endeavours, our accomplishments, our relationships, every-thing."

Language Is A Tool

That Extends Beyond

Expressing Our Wants

And Feelings Clearly.

It Is Knowing The

Effect

Our Words Have,

The Reactions

They Create,

In Our Own Minds And

In The Minds Of Others.

Robert Todd

The Laws Of Positive Language

1. LANGUAGE TRANSFERS POSITIVE AND NEGATIVE ATTITUDES.

2. WORDS AFFECT OUR BELIEF SYSTEM.

3. WORDS ARE BOTH INTERNALLY AND EXTERNALLY SPOKEN, AND AFFECT THE WAY WE FEEL.

4. STATEMENTS CHARGED WITH EMOTION HAVE INCREASED POWER.

5. POSITIVE WORDS DIRECTED TO OUR SUBCONSCIOUS CAN CREATE EVENTS IN OUR FAVOUR.

6. WORDS CREATE OUR FUTURE.

* * * * * * *

Through

Positive Language

We Can Change

Our World .

Robert Todd

Law 1

LANGUAGE TRANSFERS POSITIVE AND NEGATIVE ATTITUDES

"Words are certainly powerful, and can affect the attitudes of individuals and nations" I said, recalling the first Law of Positive Language, as we sat down to lunch at a nearby restaurant.

"I remember those speeches by Churchill during World War 2, 'We shall defend our island whatever the cost may be. We shall fight on beaches, on landing grounds, in fields, on streets, and on the hills'."

"What about his 'Finest Hour Speech'? Do you know that one?" asked Peter.

"I sure do. 'Let us brace ourselves to our duty and so bear ourselves that if the British Common-wealth lasts for a thousand years, men will still say 'This was their finest hour'."

We had a very enjoyable lunch. I was hamming it up with quotations from famous speeches and we discussed the power of words.

We ruminated on how words have been used to build empires or to destroy them, how the hypnotic wordpower of Hitler mesmerised an entire nation to fervently march to war.

We spoke with admiration of Abraham Lincoln's words "government of the people, by the people, for the people" and how these words encapsulated the aspirations of democracy in the U.S.A.

We pondered phrases such as "liberty, equality, fraternity" which epitomised the French Revolution; and "Lest we forget" which conjures up emotions of pride, anger, love, sorrow, sadness, hope and glory.

John Kennedy's "Ask not what your country can do for you. Ask what you can do for your country."

John Lennon's "Give Peace A Chance".

Lionel Ritchie and Michael Jackson's "We Are The World", under Bob Geldorf's organisation, raised millions of dollars for starving people.

We talked of the powerful effect words have on our everyday relationships, how we want to understand this power and use it wisely.

* * * * * * *

Words Have Power

I came away from that lunch more aware than ever of the powerful impact words have on the mind and the entire mental process.

WORDS HAVE TREMENDOUS POWER.

ENCOURAGEMENT

HELPS US REACH OUR GOALS.

DISCOURAGEMENT

CAN DAMPEN OUR ENDEAVOURS.

BY CHOOSING OUR WORDS,

WE CAN TRANSFORM OUR MINDS

AND THE ENVIRONMENT WE LIVE IN.

"Let's go back to the office. I have something interesting to show you" Peter said.

When we arrived at the office, I was given a book to read while Peter completed some business.

In it was a story about a school teacher who was having an appraisal visit from the District Inspector. The Inspector was becoming a little agitated because the teacher seemed to be spending too much time talking, and the Inspector had a hearty contempt for mere talk.

He asked the teacher "How can you ever change the nature of these children just by the words you speak? Show them by your deeds. Act. Don't speak. Words alone do not affect people."

The teacher wondered "What can I do to convince him?"

Finally the teacher called to one of the children "Come out to the front of the class, Tom, and grab the Inspector by the neck and push him out of the room ... ..."

On hearing those words, the Inspector protested.

The teacher said "Sir, I said only a few words. No-one pushed you, or even touched you. It was mere words. And see how it has enraged you!

Words, Sir, are very powerful."

Julie works in Peter's office. This poem sits on her desk:

> *WHEN WE SLIP AND FALL*
> *AND BREAK OUR NOSE,*
> *OR SCRATCH OUR FACE*
> *OR CUT OUR TOES*
> *WE'LL SOON BE WELL*
> *WITH DOCTOR'S CARE*
> *AND LOTS OF REST*

> *AND SUN AND AIR.*
>
> *WHEN OUR TONGUE DOES SLIP*
> *AND A CARELESS WORD*
> *BY A VULNERABLE MIND*
> *OR HEART BE HEARD*
> *THEN NO DOCTOR'S AID*
> *OR NURSE'S CARE*
> *CAN MEND THAT HEART*
> *OR MIND REPAIR.*

As well as being cute, the poem reminds us to choose carefully the words we use.

We had struck up a good relationship that first day and I felt honoured that Peter had given me so much of his time. He was particularly busy in the afternoon, and I was able to spend time thinking about the power of words and wondering if they did in fact have a tangible 'power'.

Sometimes you hear words which send a shiver down your spine, or make your skin creep, or give you a warm glow. "What is it that does this?" I wondered.

I put it to Peter.

"Words generate those feelings via the thoughts associated with them, the Rivers of Reaction" he said, "and in fact create an energy which attracts similar thoughts.

If we speak positively, we think positively. If we think positively, we attract the strong positive thoughts emanating from other people who think the same way (as a magnet draws iron filings) and we will find ourselves in positive situations as if by magic."

* * * * * * *

Pygmalion

It was another three days before I had the opportunity to talk with Peter again.

He'd told me last time that he wanted me to watch a film and, as he set it up, he said "I use this film in my training courses".

Peter left me to view the film and I settled back with positive expectations. The film was about the Pygmalion Effect.

Pygmalion was a sculptor (and the King of Cypress) in Greek legend. He carved a statue of a woman so beautiful that he fell in love with her. In answer to his prayers, and because he loved her so much, Venus the Goddess of Love turned the statue into a living woman.

George Bernard Shaw's famous book "Pygmalion", which was later the inspiration for the musical play "My Fair Lady", was based on the same concept. Professor Higgins, as a modern day Pygmalion, transformed the poor uncultured flower-seller Elisa Dolittle into a lady admired by Royalty.

"Pygmalion" is the name given to the concept that the expectation of an event can actually cause it to happen.

Look At Her,

A Prisoner Of The Gutter

Condemned

By Every Syllable She Utters .

From "Pygmalion"

By George Bernard Shaw

Professor Higgins expected to transform Eliza into a princess, and Eliza lived up to that expectation.

Another name for the Pygmalion Effect is the "self-fulfilling prophecy".

The film showed old newsreel shots of runs on certain banks during the Great Depression, to illustrate how the expectation of disaster becomes a self-fulfilling prophecy.

These runs were caused by a belief, which at the time was false, i.e. these banks were insolvent. (These particular banks were, in fact, as solvent as any other bank.) Nevertheless, they soon became insolvent as the expectation of a bank crash became a self-fulfilling prophecy.

Another example was of classroom scenes scripted along the lines of a real life experiment conducted with over 300 students. In the experiment, teachers were told that the children in their class had been tested and some of them, about 20%, had been found to have exceptional learning abilities and were expected to have remarkable intellectual growth in the next 8 months.

The children had actually been chosen at random, and the only difference between them and their classmates was in the mind of the teacher.

At the end of the school term, an I.Q. test revealed the so-called "exceptional children" had actually gained an average of 4 points more than their classmates in the I.Q. test.

The experimenter observed that the more the supposedly super-intelligent children gained in I.Q, the more the teacher liked them or favoured them, because the teacher's expectations were being fulfilled.

The amazing thing was … …

The other children in the class who gained significantly in I.Q., especially if they had been labelled slow learners, were treated less favourably by the teacher on an intellectual basis, and also with regard to social and emotional barriers as well.

The teacher seemed to prefer the students to behave as expected.

The experiment group children all bloomed because of their teacher's expectations, and the teacher treated them favourably because of their achievements.

Some of the others bloomed as well, yet in this case the teacher failed to give them favourable treatment because they had behaved differently from expectations.

The scene shifted to a training centre for the unemployed.

The welding teacher was told that a few of his trainees had a high aptitude for welding. In fact, they were chosen at random.

During the six months of the course, the selected people changed their behaviour significantly. Their attendance at class was more regular than the others in the control group. They gained the skills of welding in little more than half the time of their fellow trainees. At the completion of the course, they scored an average of 10 points higher in comprehensive welding tests.

The experimenter asked the trainees to do a rating on themselves and their classmates. Without exception, each trainee chose the selected few as the people they would like to work with.

When the instructor was told the purpose of the experiment, he was amazed. He believed he had spoken and acted in the same way with all the trainees. The instructor's expectation was the only independent variable in the experiment. His beliefs had influenced the performance of the selected trainees, and his language had created a self-fulfilling prophecy.

Peter returned as the film ended, and asked what I thought of it.

"Very good" I answered. "I learned about the Pygmalion Effect, how our expectations can affect other people, and how the expectations of others can influence us."

"Can you see how language has a great Pygmalion Effect on people?" Peter asked.

"Yes, I can."

"Eliza Dolittle being passed off as a great lady is a perfect example of this" said Peter.

"We expect a certain type of language from a certain type of person, and the words we use transfer positive or negative expectations.

People carry around with them beliefs, which have been programmed into them by words delivered from 'on high' by their parents, teachers, peers, limiting their abilities or expanding them. They have come to believe that other people's forecasts are what is expected of them."

* * * * * * *

Self And Positive Language

It was a warm, sunny day and I felt good. I parked the car and strolled through the shopping centre on my way to our next meeting.

We were holding the meetings regularly now. I looked forward to them, and was definitely feeling more positive.

Today we were going to talk about me.

"Do you think people in general use more negative language than positive talk, Peter?"

"Overwhelmingly so. Surveys have revealed that the average person thinks negatively 77% of the time, and that leaves a lot of room for improvement.

That's why people who use positive language are so successful. They understand the power of positive language. Doorways to opportunity open to them as if by magic … …"

... The Words We Use

Have A Magical Effect

On Us

As We Use Them .

Aldous Huxley

"Most people's minds are too full of negative influences to be attracted by positive opportunities. Their minds are full of FAILURE PHRASES and BARRIER PHRASES, which are in fact negative affirmations.

Failure Phrases are negative statements people make about themselves; and if they were true, or were to become true, it would be to their detriment.

These self critical words are impressed at the subconscious level.

Every time you call yourself '*hopeless*' or '*a fool*'; every time you put yourself down, even if it's a joke; you are programming it, at the subconscious level.

Some typical Failure Phrases are:

> I'm a dreadful cook.
> I haven't got much colour sense.
> Who would have me in their team?
> I'm a lousy e-mail writer.
> My memory is getting worse.
> Why does it always happen to me?"

"Barrier Phrases, on the other hand, limit us and create obstacles. Some examples are:

> I'm no good in the morning until I have a cup of coffee.
> I was out late last night, so I won't have any energy today.
> When I have to use the computer, I get confused.
> When I have a lot of homework, I get headaches."

I asked "Do statements such as *'I'm no good in the morning until I've had a cup of coffee'* scour a habit track in our subconscious, and create a self-fulfilling prophecy?"

"Barrier Phrases are conditional. In other words, until the person has a cup of coffee, the subconscious mind is almost compelled to fulfil the statement 'I am no good in the morning'.

By repeating a Barrier Phrase over and over, the impact of the words goes even deeper. It becomes a negative Affirmation. We are programming our mind to fulfil the statement. In fact, any statement we make repeatedly, is impressed on the subconscious, and can become a self-fulfilling prophecy, therefore any repetitive statements negative to yourself are better eliminated ... ..."

...... If You Say It,

You Think It .

When You Eliminate It

From Your

Verbal Vocabulary,

You Eliminate It

From Your

Thinking Vocabulary .

Robert Todd

"Statements such as *'Anything I eat goes to fat'* or *'No matter what I eat, I put on weight'* have a great affect on our metabolism. The mind controls the body and therefore controls the weight.

Other phrases we want to eliminate, because there's no place in positive language for superfluous words. Saying things like *'at this point in time'* instead of *'now'* is waffling. Use one word instead of a phrase whenever possible.

Also, eliminate words that diminish your integrity. Phrases such as *'to tell you the truth'* or *'I'm being honest about this'* or *'frankly speaking'* imply that you are not always honest or truthful.

Be honest. A positive person is truthful at all times. In fact, it's a pre-requisite to understanding the power of positive language.

It is important that you tell the truth because, if your mind becomes accustomed to lies, it will not recognise the truth.

If you are truthful, you will recognise lies immediately. You will be aware of what is going on, and other people will be unable to take advantage of you.

In negotiation, we use the expression 'Listen carefully; trust others; and check all'."

"This does not mean that if someone tells you a lie, you call them a liar (the positive person is tactful and patient). You wait for the right moment, then guide them to the understanding that the truth is a better long term way to achieve their goals.

Dishonest people do not like to be around honest people, because they know their stories do not work.

If you are unaware of an answer, say so. Eliminate *'I'm not sure'* or *'I'm not certain about that'*. When you are asked if you know the answer, say 'yes' or 'no', or 'I've heard a little about it, please fill me in' or 'I'll do some research and get back to you'.

Another phrase to eliminate is *'with all due respect'*. It usually means you're not going to show any - and that there is criticism coming.

Also we remove words that judge, criticise and condemn, or compare yourself with others."

"That's interesting, Peter. Why is it so important to avoid using the particular words that judge, evaluate, label and compare?"

Peter thought about my question before replying, and then said "Because you are building limits on yourself."

"If you call yourself a 'housewife, builder, accountant' or anything else, this tends to limit your potential outside these areas. So, when you talk about yourself, rather than limit yourself with a label, talk about your skills and abilities.

You are a unique person with unique talents. Use these abilities to best advantage. It is better to be yourself - not like anyone else.

Also, in carrying out a task, you do not *'succeed'* or *'fail'*, it is 'succeed' or 'discover'. When things do not go as expected, you will discover areas you want to learn or improve to accomplish your goal.

If you feel you have a weakness in a particular area, remember you have different abilities and experiences which others do not have. Use these experiences to guide you toward your goals.

For example, if a meal you cook is not successful, rather than '*I am a lousy cook*' you say 'the meal could have been cooked better. The next time I will ... ... (and state what you will do to accomplish the goal)'. This way, you have directed any comments at the task, instead of yourself.

This is like a famous inventor who, after he created a new product, was asked by one of his students 'It must have been hard to keep going when you had 919 failures?'"

"He replied 'Failures! I've successfully discovered 919 ways it won't work, and one that will."

I made a resolution to eliminate Failure Phrases, Barrier Phrases, and self-criticism, from my own language.

"If words can actually affect us physically, as well as making a blueprint for what's expected, then we must be especially careful how we speak with our children?"

* * * * * * *

The Secret

Of Being Positive Is

To Keep Your Attention

On All Subjects Positively

And Express Them In

Positive Language

Robert Todd

Children And Positive Language

"From an early age" said Peter, "as the child begins to establish some sort of order out of their environment and make sense of the world, they establish a blueprint for their lives.

A child feels inferior under the influence of older people, and sees them as the source of all knowledge and wisdom, the all-knowing, all-wise ones.

This is the position we hold as very young children. Regardless of how much loving we receive, we are very vulnerable little people in a world full of giants, who support us, yet admonish us.

It wasn't all confidence lowering. We were built up by the loving we were receiving. Even the simple act of being picked up and fed was good for our feelings of self worth.

If our parents are gentle, nurturing and highly communicative with us, that goes into our blueprint, into our psychological script, and we tend to be the same style of parent when we grow up.

If they are harsh and punitive, or judgmental, or bigoted, or over-protective, those characteristics are in our script."

"For some of us, this script can bring us contentment and success; for others, misery and failure.

Words play a very important role in the formation of our script.

The golden rule is to treat children as individuals, not compare them with anyone else."

"What if they ask 'Who am I like'?" I questioned "because children seem to ask this."

"Answer 'You are like you. And you are very unique'.

We must not compare a child to anyone else, for they will observe that person and take on their negative characteristics as well as their positive ones."

"Well, what about the practice of correcting our children?" I asked.

"Let's imagine you are 3 years old. You have a 5 year old brother who has just started school.

On the first day, he brings home this fantastic finger painting. You know it's fantastic because when mum sees it, she puts it on the fridge, the pride of place for everyone to see."

"You figure that you could do as well, so you head into your room, get some of your brother's paints, and do a painting. You present it to your brother.

He looks at it and says '*It's a mess.*' He crumples it up and says '*You can't paint. You're hopeless.*' You walk away realising you just can't paint, and you're hopeless.

You practise painting in your room, not showing your brother or anyone else, because you know you can't paint.

At the age of 4, you think now is your chance.

Out in the yard, your brother is playing with his friends. So you spend some time doing a painting, carefully this time, making sure you use all the colours you feel are right.

You take this great painting out to your brother. You want to impress his mates and become friends. Your brother takes the painting over to his mates. They start laughing and saying things like '*See, he couldn't even keep in the lines*! *Have you ever seen a green man?*'

This creates embarrassment, and you realise the act you've carried out to win friends, has caused you to lose them. So now, you really know that painting is not your forte."

"Some weeks later, you think 'Maybe mum will be a little more sympathetic'. You spend some time in your room creating a masterpiece, and then head down to get mum.

Mum walks into your room, looks and says '*What on earth have you done, you stupid child*? Get that off the wall immediately!' And she gives you a clout over the ear.

Now you have learned that painting is downright dangerous, you're hopeless, and it causes you to lose your friends."

"Are these critical statements and actions impressed at the subconscious level of the child?" I asked.

"Yes" replied Peter. "Telling a child *they are hopeless at something*, or that *they will achieve very little*, sets up an expectation in them which can become a self-fulfilling prophecy. We must comment on their actions, and not their characteristics.

By saying '*You're a naughty, bad, or stupid, boy or girl*' we create in the child's mind both an image and a feeling of themselves as bad, stupid, or naughty. These words describe a character-istic or behaviour pattern of the child, and the child tends to live up to the expectation, therefore they have to be avoided."

"If a child says '*I can't do it* - and you believe they can - to contradict the child encourages them to prove you wrong. It is far more effective to move a child progressively through a series of statements from 'I can't do it' to 'I don't want to' (it is all right to allow the child to have this opinion, and it is necessary for you to find out the reason they don't want to), next, to 'I can if I want to' and finally 'I want to and I can'.

Children occasionally do things wrong or make mistakes, so if we use the word '*wrong*' or '*mistake*', such as 'that was the wrong thing to do' or 'that was a mistake', the words indicate to the child that they could have achieved their goal another way, the correct way.

If the child is doing something wrong, you say 'stop' and tell them the correct thing to do.

For example, if a child is playing with a power point which is dangerous, you could say 'Stop! That is made for plugs! If you want to play with something, play with one of your toys.' Then, distract the child with their toys.

If a child is pulling saucepans out of the cupboard while a parent is cooking dinner, many parents say '*You can't do that while I am cooking*' and shut the cupboard door. Almost automatically, the child will think 'I know I can do that' and will be drawn back to pulling out the saucepans."

"Whereas, if the parent had said 'Stop. Play with your toys while I am cooking dinner', it is more likely the child will be distracted and play with their toys."

"That's O.K. What about dealing with a child who throws a tantrum in the middle of the kitchen floor?" I asked.

"When I was very young, I remember watching a child throw a tantrum. The wise mother took no notice and deliberately walked past the child, then accidentally on purpose bumped the child gently with her foot, then turned around and trod lightly on his fingers, more to scare than to hurt.

The tantrum stopped. The child looked up and said 'You kicked me and trod on my fingers'. The mother replied 'Well, if you lie in the middle of the floor kicking, you are smart enough to know you must put up with the consequences'.

The child very quickly learned that tantrums were ineffective, and therefore not the way to achieve a goal. Consequently the tantrums stopped."

"So, the parent won and the child lost" I said.

"Nobody won; the child learned" Peter replied.

"With children, it's important to avoid terms such as *'win'* or *'lose'*; we can say 'win' or 'learn'."

"When a child is unsuccessful, it highlights the skills they must learn or practise to achieve the goal. If someone else is better, they may have practised more, or be talented in that particular field.

If the child is not highly skilled in an area, it is important to remind them that everyone is different - they have abilities in other areas.

Do not compare weaknesses. Concentrate on the child's strengths and uniqueness. Each ability is as important as another. No child is better than; they are different to."

"That's interesting" I said. "Can you tell me about praising children?"

"I believe children thrive on praise and, if the child is behaving in the correct manner, then you praise them and tell them how well they have done.

If you notice certain talents or characteristics in the child, you reinforce these with positive statements.

Telling children they have a good head for figures, or they'd make a good doctor, or can write a good story, or they have a good memory, or can sell ice to Eskimos, can also become a self-fulfilling prophecy."

"Whether you are a parent dealing with children, interacting with your family and friends, or a manager dealing with adults, it is important to realise the impact you are having on them with the words you use."

* * * * * * *

Do Not Let

What You Cannot Do,

Interfere With

What You Can Do .

John Wooden

By Choosing

The Appropriate Words,

It Is Possible

To Transform The Mind

Of An Individual.

Robert Todd

Law 2

WORDS AFFECT OUR BELIEF SYSTEM

"Each of us has different Belief Systems, and these form the basis of how we perceive the world we live in, and the codes for achieving our goals. We have learned these Belief Patterns by listening to, and observing, those around us - our parents, our teachers, our religions, our schools, our culture.

These Belief Systems are developed to enable us to understand life, to cope, and they are the basis for our goals and decision-making.

Emotions, such as love, hate, fear, contentment, greed, jealousy, are developed by our environment and by those around us. The goals we want to achieve, are the goals that we have been taught are correct for us, and are important in our life.

Because of what we have been told, we sometimes attempt to achieve possessions, or create situations so we can achieve particular feelings to fulfil our Belief Patterns."

"Are you saying that many of these concepts are handed down through the ages?" I asked.

"Yes. They have been transferred to us through language, and have become the foundations of many of the Proverbs and Truisms that are transferred from generation to generation.

Many of these Truisms and Proverbs were in fact excuses, which have become codes of life and predictions for the future, and can create a self-fulfilling prophecy. Some of them are negative, and create limitations on our potential."

I wondered how so-called Truisms create limit-ations in the mind. I posed this question to Peter.

* * * * * * *

Proverbs And Truisms

"I am sure you know many people who say *'It's too good to be true'* or *'I have no right to have it so good'* or *'It can't last'*.

They are programming their mind to have things go wrong. And when it does, they say *'You must have the bad to appreciate the good'* or *'Win some, lose some'* or *'I told you so'*.

I noticed that you used a lot of these statements when talking about your business, Thomas. I suggest that you be vigilant in what you say, and look at the effect these statements can have on your life and your business.

Many of your decisions are based on sayings or situations which were Culturally Imposed or People Imposed, and have become part of your Belief System. And many of the situations that exist in organisations, families, or relationships, are in fact Imposed Barriers or Limitations.

You may know someone who is absolutely time conscious. They feel they must always be on time.

This can come about because they were told that it was wrong to be late."

"Maybe when they were a child, they arrived late to the table, and were punished; or maybe they were late for sport, and were stopped from playing.

They have learned that if they are late, something bad is going to happen. This is often referred to as 'Fear Training'.

Later in life, the particular incident that created the programme may be forgotten, yet if they are travelling for work and the train comes late, they become agitated. Their mind is saying 'I'm late. Something bad is going to happen'.

If the person is also money conscious, this could stimulate the Truism *'Time is money'* or create a personal Truism of *'Don't be late, or you'll miss the boat'*.

This affects the individual. However there are proverbs which create situations between people.

For example, the Proverbs *'Look before you leap'* or *'Fools rush in where angels fear to tread'* tell us that we must hesitate before we move, or something bad will happen.

The alternatives, *'He who hesitates is lost'* or *'A stitch in time saves nine'*, instil in us that we must move quickly to achieve our goals, or something bad will happen."

"In a relationship, if one person believes *'Look before you leap'* and another believes *'He who hesitates is lost'*, when it comes to decision making, this creates tension - one wants to hesitate, and the other wants to move.

Money is another area where it is interesting to notice the effect of Proverbs and Truisms on people.

In many courses I conduct, I ask the group how many of them want a million dollars.

Inevitably there are a number of people, approximately 1 in 12, who do not want that much money. Some say it would change them too much, others say it would be too much responsibility, while others say they would not know what to do with it.

Logically, they could take the million dollars and give most of it away, except they would then feel some inner guilt, so they would rather not have it in the first place. Obviously they have some in-built belief which creates a rejection of money.

This is understandable because we have many statements such as *'Money is the root of all evil', 'Money doesn't grow on trees', 'Honest people are poor', 'Poor people are happy', 'Something that comes easily is not worth having', 'You can't be a millionaire without hard work'.*"

"Have you heard these, Thomas?"

"Yes" I said. "And I have heard that many people who win lotto, or the lottery, are bankrupt within two years. I suppose this is because they can't change their way of thinking and attitudes towards money."

"When any of these beliefs are prevalent in our mind" Peter continued "they create a limit beyond which people cannot move without some feeling of guilt or doubt.

Many of our Cultural attitudes, philosophies or idiologies, restrict our thinking, and limit us from taking opportunities.

I believe it is important that we challenge these Proverbs and Truisms because, as we have seen, many of them contradict each other. It's important, if you say them, to realise that they will have an effect on your life. You must decide for yourself which ones you want to be true for you.

What are some Proverbs and Truisms you can think of, Thomas, apart from the ones I have already mentioned?"

"The Proverbs that readily come to my mind are:

> Bad luck comes in threes.
> The early bird catches the worm.
> First in, best dressed.
> There is the quick or the dead.
> You can't count your chickens by breaking eggs.
> Patience is a virtue, possess it if you can.
> You can't win them all.
> When all else fails, read the instructions.
> If you don't know now, you never will.
> There are no short cuts to success.
> Two heads are better than one.
> You can't get there from here.
> No pain, no gain.
> Wear clean underwear in case you get hit by a bus.
> The good old days.
> I was better off when … …"

"Some of these statements seem to be a habit in my life. How do I change them?" I asked.

"Before I answer that question, I would like to make a comment on some of the statements, and what I'm about to tell you applies to all statements of this type.

Firstly, '*Bad luck comes in threes*' means that, if something bad happens, you start looking for two more events to fulfil the proverb.

'*Two heads are better than one*' says that you will make better decisions with someone else's help.

'*No gain, no pain*' means that you cannot move forward unless you suffer.

And the last one you mentioned '*I was better off when ... ...*' instils in your mind that the future will not be as enjoyable as the past, unless the same conditions re-occur.

Be very careful if you are using statements such as these.

Whenever you say one of these so-called Truisms, stop for a moment and say to yourself 'Do I want this to be true in my life? Will this help me achieve my goals'?"

Proverbs and Truisms 87

"If the answer is in the affirmative, then keep the statement in your vocabulary.

If you are unsure, or believe the statement is negative, then consciously discard it, avoid dwelling on it, for this gives is reinforcement. Counteract it with a statement that will help you achieve your goals."

* * * * * * *

Unless You Consciously

Feed Your Mind

With Positive Statements,

Others Will Fill It

With Negative Ones .

Robert Todd

Law 3

WORDS ARE BOTH INTERNALLY

AND EXTERNALLY SPOKEN,

AND AFFECT THE WAY WE FEEL.

"To explain this Law, I'd like you to say the words 'poisonous spider'. Say it to yourself two or three times, then allow whatever image comes into your mind to accompany the words. Keep the words and the image together, as you visualise the spider moving towards you right now.

Now say 'delicious hot dinner'. Say it three times. Imagine having just completed a delicious hot dinner. You're sitting at the table with your friends or family, relaxed and content.

When you said 'poisonous spider' and visualised the spider coming towards you, you probably had a little anxious feeling.

When you said 'delicious hot dinner', it brought back familiar feelings you'd experienced of delicious hot dinners. If you were especially hungry, it might even make your stomach react or your mouth water.

In these examples, you've called into play the three brain languages - verbal, visual and kinesthetic (feelings)."

"These three languages are used simultaneously every time a thought occurs.

If you spend more time talking about delicious meals than poisonous spiders, you will experience more good feelings than bad ones.

When you were born, as you had no language, you relied upon emotions. This was the way you dealt with life - you 'felt' what was going on.

When the light was shining brightly in your eyes, you shut your eyes or cried. And when you heard something loud, you cried."

"The next stage was visualising, and the realisation that when a certain image came into view, it was associated with your present feeling.

In the third stage, you learned language so you could refer to what was annoying you.

First came feelings, then images, then words: this is referred to as '3 D Thinking'.

Later on in life, you can move from one to the others:

> Feelings triggered words and images.
> Images triggered words and feelings.
> Words triggered images and feelings.

As adults, we can choose the words we use, therefore we can affect the feelings of ourselves and others. So ... ..."

... ... Every Time You Say

Positive Words,

You Simultaneously

Visualise Positive Images

And Experience

Positive Feelings .

That Is Why It's Important

To Use Positive Language

At All Times .

Robert Todd

This was a real revelation to me, that words automatically trigger feelings. I realised this is the reason I felt better about someone saying to me "You're right" instead of "You're not wrong".

I put it to Peter.

"That's it, Thomas, you've got it" said Peter. "The more you use positive success statements rather than negative failure statements, the better you'll feel and the more successful you'll become. So drop words with negative connocations, and speak positively. Replace negative statements with positive ones, and feel much better."

"Peter, it seems to me that this Law *Words are both internally and externally spoken, and affect the way we feel* is very powerful."

"It's certainly powerful" he said. "All the Laws are important."

"Before we discuss the other Laws, could I ask you some more questions about this one?

If people with illnesses realised this, they would automatically feel a little better each time they used positive language."

* * * * * *

I Choose To Be

Healthy And Free .

All Is Well

In My World .

Louise L. Hay

Health

"Health and language go hand in hand" Peter said. "The words we say can control or eliminate many illnesses, and promote good health. Our attitude towards health is often Culturally Imposed and relative to the language and attitudes of our family.

I believe the health messages parents give their children have a great impact on them throughout their lives and, when they grow up and become parents, there is a strong subconscious preference to transfer the same messages to their children.

These days, more than ever, the medical profession believes that maintaining a positive mental attitude is one of the most vital aspects to assist in the healing process. If we talk negatively or think negatively about health, it appears we actually affect our immune system."

"I remember the experience of a friend of mine" I said. "His father died at the age of 42. Two years later, his uncle died at the age of 42. This person had two male members of his family who died at the same age.

His mother believed that he could develop a heart problem the same as his father, so he was sent to a specialist who examined him thoroughly."

"The doctor came to the conclusion that his heart was as strong as a long distance runner. Yet every time he became tired, whether it was caused by sport or staying our late, his mother would continually say *'Take it easy. Don't strain yourself. You don't want heart problems like your father'*.

He was advised by his mother to take on a simple job to avoid worry, and told not to accept promotion on the basis that *'It was the strain and stress of the job that killed your father'*.

So, from the time his father had died, until he was over 42, even though he had been examined earlier by specialists, each time he attempted to exert himself, there was concern and almost a fear that he could develop heart problems the same as his father.

As worry can cause heart problems, he could have developed the same complaint as his father.

I wonder how many people go through life worrying about the fact that they may inherit an illness and, by the sheer worry of that fact, they create the illness?"

"I am sure many do" replied Peter. "In fact, in the book 'Love Your Disease - It's Keeping You Healthy' which was written by Dr John Harrison. He says that he believes disease is both self-created and self-cured."

"In a nutshell, Dr Harrison believes we choose a disease because of the advantages illness can bring us - attention, love, solitude, respite from work, etc. He says that, by being ill, we care for our inner wants. He also believes pre-disposition to a disease is often passed on (not in a physical sense, that is, through transmission of faulty genes) through the messages parents give their offspring, also the living habits and diet they pass down.

The more we use positive language, and reinforce positive beliefs with our language, the more we will enjoy good health.

If you frequently say *'I seem unable to cope these days'* or *'Everything is getting on top of me'* or *'I seem to be depressed all the time'* or *'Everything irritates me'* or *'I seem to be having more illness'*, then you are programming your mind to create these situations.

I believe many people who suffer illness, have created the illness by the language they use, therefore they could reduce the effects - and in many cases cure the illness - by adopting positive language.

For many years doctors have told us that if we are in a job where there is stress or worry, we are likely to create heart troubles or develop an ulcer."

"Incorrect attitude or language can create anxieties and frustration. Therefore, once we understand how to move into a positive environment through the use of positive language, obviously we will diminish the stress placed on us, and start to alleviate many of the illnesses we suffer.

I am not suggesting that you avoid consulting a medical practitioner, if you believe it is necessary. I am suggesting that you can support the healing process by your attitude and language.

I often hear people say things like *'He makes me sick'* or *'It makes me ill when I think of it'* or *'I'll never survive without ... ...'* or *'I'm dying to get there'*.

All these types of statements can be removed from our vocabulary, as it is important, when we use positive language, that we use it in all aspects of our life, including health.

I know parents who say to their children *'If you eat that, you'll be sick'* or *'If you go outside without a jumper, you'll get a cold'*. It is better to advise children what is right, rather than threaten them with something that is wrong ... ..."

"If you listen to people when they are discussing the common cold, they make statements such as *'When there's a change in the weather, I get a cold'*, *'If there are colds going around the office, I'm sure to get one'* or *'I have been sitting next to someone who has a cold, so I will get one, for sure'*, *'Air conditioners always affect me'*. If our language can affect the immune system, then obviously we become vulnerable to illness.

On the other hand if we believe, as many people do, that they are always healthy, it seems they can go for of years without ever being affected by the illnesses going around.

In courses that I conduct, if I have someone who has a cold, I usually ask them to come to the front of the room. This way, people do not start thinking *'The person behind keeps coughing on me and I'm likely to get a cold'*.

In the last 20 years, while I've been training, I use the statement 'I am always healthy'. I have conducted every session I have booked, and only on 2 occasions have I had a very slight cough.

Other trainers frequently say to me 'How come your voice survives? After a day lecturing, I find my voice is becoming hoarse, and yet you seem to be have the ability to talk all day without any effect'?"

"In fact, I conduct some courses for five days. I talk most of the time, either lecturing, in discussion, or talking to individuals, and I find my voice is quite capable of handling this. I believe this is because I have always stated that 'my voice is always in good condition'."

"So, if I say *'I never get sick'* I would improve my health?" I asked.

"If you say *'I never get sick'* you are breaking the rules of positive language by using the words *'never'* and *'sick'*. Therefore it is important that you express it positively by saying 'I am always healthy'.

This concept is not new, when it comes to health.

One of the most famous exponents of language and health was a French pharmacist by the name of Emile Coue. He successfully used the power of suggestion to cure patients.

I'm sure you know his most famous saying which was 'Every day in every way, I'm getting better and better'. He asked his patients to say this over and over again in a relaxed way until it seeped into the subconscious mind and became a part of their belief system.

He healed many patients that other doctors had given up."

"People who continually talk of the good old days, and discuss everyone else's poor health, or how many of their friends are now suffering illness because of their age, if they associate age with illness, and read articles, and discuss how when people get older, their memories get worse, their hearing and eyes (or anything else) start to fail, they are creating a self-fulfilling prophecy for themself.

Alternatively, there are many cases of people being cured from cancer in what is referred to as 'spontaneous remission'. Doctors do not understand how - yet they know it happens. Many doctors these days believe that this type of remission takes place because of the attitude and beliefs of the patient. As attitudes and beliefs are developed through language, I believe each word we say is vital.

A good book on this subject is 'Getting Well Again' by Dr Carl Simonton.

Another interesting book on healing, that is worth reading, is 'You Can Heal Your Life' by Louise Hay, who also recommends the use of Affirmations.

I believe that reading these books will be of great benefit to you. They explain in detail the theory of how words can be used to improve health."

* * * * * * *

Every Day

In Every Way

I'm Getting

Better And Better

Emil Coue

Self Talk

"Let us imagine you have a dental appointment, you may sit in the dentist's waiting room thinking '*I hope it doesn't hurt too much. I hate dentists*' or maybe '*I wonder if the dentist will find any holes*'.

This chatter in your head is referred to as Self Talk.

There is, of course, positive and negative Self Talk. Positive Self Talk moves you towards your goals. Negative Self Talk moves you away from your goals.

When a negative person fails at some activity, they have a tendency to use negative Self Talk, such as '*That's like me*'. When they succeed, they tend to think '*That's unusual for me*' or '*It's just a fluke*'.

Using Self Talk which is de-motivational, can create recurring failure.

It has been shown that positive people, when they do something right, tend to think 'That's like me. I did that very well', or 'Good job.' And, when they do not achieve the success they desire, they think 'That's unusual for me. From now on, I intend to ... ...' or 'What have I learned? The next time I'll ... ...'"

"This programmes the mind, and stimulates it to move towards success. Use positive Self Talk, and continually motivate yourself towards your goals.

Become aware of, and control, your Self Talk. What you think to yourself and what you believe will, in fact, become reality.

Often people have a conflict in their minds '*I am; I'm not. I am; I'm not. I am; I'm not*'. This is why it is important you modify any Self Talk that is not moving you towards your goals, into a language which is positive and will move you towards attaining your objectives.

People who have difficulty getting up in the morning say to themself '*I have difficulty getting up in the morning*' or '*I'm always late*' or '*I sleep in and I don't hear the alarm clock*' and other negative Self Talk.

Start looking at what you would be, if everything were ideal.

For example 'I wake up refreshed in the morning' or 'I hear the alarm clock and am fully awake' or 'I wake up and get up', whatever you want as the final result. How would you describe yourself when you have made the change?

Generally we keep this to one sentence."

"It is a good idea to write out the positive Self Talk you want, and read it a few times each day until it is a habit.

Whenever you realise you are using negative Self Talk, change it to positive statements. Then add to your Self Talk, positive feelings of success. This gives it greater power.

For example, you decide to use the positive Self Talk 'I get up refreshed in the morning'. Visualise yourself doing that, and add the feeling of how you would feel when you get up feeling refreshed.

Once you have developed Self Talk for a particular task, monitor it each time you carry out the task, to ensure you are keeping yourself on track.

Let's say answering the telephone, your new Self Talk could be 'I handle phone calls quickly and easily'. The phone rings. As you reach for the phone, think your Self Talk statement. Then visualise yourself handling calls easily, and feel the emotion of accomplishment.

When you follow the three steps - Self Talk, images, and feelings - you will find this is very powerful."

****

People Speak Confidently

Because

They Are Successful

And

People Are Successful

Because

They Speak Confidently

Robert Todd

Law 4

STATEMENTS CHARGED WITH EMOTION

HAVE INCREASED POWER

Every time you speak, you also visualise and feel the associated emotions.

A statement on its own has no power - it is just words. It is the associated image and feeling that gives it power. The clearer the image, the stronger the feeling, the greater the power.

Anyone can say they will climb Mount Everest, yet only those who say and believe it - the ones who can see and feel the success - are the ones who will succeed. They have the commitment and the belief.

Whatever you can perceive and believe, can become reality.

Belief is the power. First of all, believe in yourself, believe in what you can do. Grasp the concept of your infinite ability, widen your boundaries as far as you can imagine them to be. Say, see, and feel success, then add your commitment and belief.

* * * * * * *

POSITIVE LANGUAGE

IS THE KEY TO

POSITIVE THINKING .

BELIEF IS THE POWER

THAT TURNS THE KEY .

Robert Todd

Imagination And Belief

"Peter, why is it so difficult for people to be positive? I understand that negative forces are dominant in our environment, in the general expressions people use, and in the media's daily pronouncements. I understand that it takes discipline and hard work to fight our negative environment.

Why do some people have a fear of, or won't even consider, that a positive attitude could change their lives? What are your thoughts on this?

The usual comments I hear from people who won't embrace the philosophy of positivity and who therefore won't begin to use positive language are:

… …   We are only fooling ourselves if we think talking positively and expecting good things to happen can actually make them happen.

or …   By substituting 'I'm a kind, loving person' for 'I'm a bad person whom no one likes' and expecting to change some of our character, is ridiculous.

or …   I guess I look at things in a negative way, but I can't change my personality."

"or ...   I believe your philosophy intellectually, but not emotionally.

or ...   The words you use in positive language describe a situation unrealistically.

or ...   Why can't I say 'I want to earn $500,000 a year' and have it come true?

or ...   (even more ridiculous) Why can't I jump from a 10 storey building after saying to myself 'I'll land safely on the ground'?

What are your answers to these people, Peter?"

"I agree with them."

"You agree with them?"

"Yes, Thomas, for them it's true. You see, under-standing positive language is the key to being positive, and the power that turns the key is belief.

Their belief system is their understanding of the world, based on all their experiences and influences of the past.

So, whatever they perceive and believe, is their reality, and as we've discussed before, the limitations are the limitations they place upon themselves."

They Have To Understand

The Principle

Whatever You Can

Perceive And Believe,

Can Become Reality .

"What about the person jumping off the building?" I asked. "You can't expect them to imagine jumping 10 storeys and expecting to survive the fall?"

"Of course not. The point is, they know they can't do it, and they can't imagine themselves doing it.

Such people bring up these objections simply to prove to themselves that the theory is wrong. If they can disprove the theory, then obviously being positive doesn't work - and therefore it won't work in any situation."

"I ask these people to tell me their objective. They say 'to jump off the building and land safely'. If you think positively, this is easy, because as far as jumping from high buildings is concerned, many people have taken on this challenge - and come up with parachutes, gliding or abseiling; and the negative people still say this is simply a way out, and claim that it doesn't change the concept.

If we really want to have a look at people who are positive, you have only to think of the movie industry where stuntmen have come up with ways to jump off a building, flap their arms and land safely. Some have used the concept of a wire to restrict the fall, others have jumped off 10 storey buildings with air bags and landed safely. The latest trend is to jump off 50 metre high bridges with bungy ropes.

Being positive doesn't break the laws of nature. It enables us to come up with methods and answers of using these laws to achieve things which in many cases appear impossible. People restrict their beliefs, and therefore restrict the answers they can achieve.

I suppose there are some people who, no matter what you say or how you look at things, will believe only what they want to believe. They will still claim that you can't jump off a building and land safely, although the examples I have given you explain how this can be done."

"Again, with earning big money, if you can't imagine yourself earning $500,000 a year, there is no point talking about it (although many men and women earn this type of income).

If you can't imagine, or don't believe you can be a kind loving person, then there is no point talking about it."

"How do you answer the person who said they accept your theory intellectually, yet not emotionally?"

"People often confuse the terms 'thinking' and 'feeling.' You hear people say I 'feel' you are wrong, instead of I 'believe' you are wrong. Usually when people say 'feel' in a case such as this, they are expressing a degree of belief.

If you are to receive the full benefit of positive language, you must believe in it. Positive language is a very powerful means of getting whatever you want in life."

* * * * * * *

Whatever You Can Do

Or Dream You Can,

Begin It .

Boldness Has Genius,

Magic

And Power In It .

Begin It Now .

Johann Wolfgang Goethe

Praise Phrases

My meetings with Peter over the past couple of weeks had made a strong effect on me.

I've started to listen more, and to observe the effectiveness of particular words.

I've learned to use "and" instead of "but", or sometimes eliminate "but" altogether. I've noticed how "but" puts two ideas or opinions in opposition to each other and devalues one of them. When we say "and" then both ideas can exist simultaneously.

Good manners have a softening effect on people, as do words like INVITE which are used to encourage co-operation.

It seems that when you tell somebody what to do, they don't want to do it. If you invite them to do it, it's a different story.

I noticed at conferences, after morning tea, if someone says "It's time to begin" there's resistance. If they say "I want you to return to the room" the resistance is stronger.

"I invite you to come back into the room" produces a much more favourable reaction.

Another softening effect that works, is to use what I call PRAISE PHRASES; that is, to say positive, encouraging phrases that mirror your genuine interest and liking for another person.

It seems to be part of our culture that giving or receiving compliments is embarrassing, and I have noticed that many people seem to shrug off any praise that is given. It is important that you be generous with praise.

Alternatively, if someone gives you a compliment, it is not necessary to make a issue of it. A polite "thank you" shows you recognise their comment and appreciate it, without being over-egotistical.

Actual Praise Phrases differ with each situation. One has to learn about another person's business, interests or hobbies, so that you can genuinely compliment them on their achievements or talk with them about their particular field. Use only genuine heart-felt interest which is transferred by the words we use.

Make sincere compliments to others. The amazing thing is that the more you give, the more you get.

Be on the lookout for a way to genuinely compliment people.

A simple and interesting way to compliment your family and friends is, when they are carrying out an activity - such as cooking, sewing, repairing the house or car - every so often you observe their activity and compliment them on how well they are doing, how good it looks, and how brilliant and successful they are, at carrying out the activity.

INTERNAL Praise Phrases are important too.

Catch yourself doing something well and give yourself a sincere compliment. Take credit for the good things you do and the good things that happen to you.

WELL DONE !

CONGRATULATIONS !

THAT'S A GREAT IDEA !

Praise yourself internally, and others externally. Use Praise Phrases as often as you can. They create positive vibrations within yourself and others.

I find too that asking for advice creates positive vibes between people.

When you ask for advice, you are complimenting people and recognising the value of their opinion.

Most people are very willing and genuine in their help and advice. Remember to thank them for their opinion, and advise them of the result.

The way to gain rapport with another person is to be genuinely interested in that person.

* * * * * *

Law 5

POSITIVE WORDS DIRECTED TO

OUR SUBCONSCIOUS CAN CREATE

EVENTS IN OUR FAVOUR

Our subconscious has a vast repertoire of sayings, comments, thoughts, and beliefs, that we have collected over our lifetime. When triggered, sometimes many years later, they can create positive or negative reactions.

We act on situations, rather than react to situations.

As you become aware that you are reacting negatively, because of a negative programme, you can change it by over-printing. The easiest way to do this, is - stop and ask yourself "What is my goal?" and "How do I act positively in this situation to achieve that goal?"

Changing an outside activity is not enough. We must re-programme the subconscious, by using words in a particular way, to achieve the desired response and direct events in our favour.

By changing your language and using Affirmations, you can over-print the previous programme to gain control of your life.

* * * * * * *

To Be

Positive Outside,

Be

Positive Inside .

Robert Todd

Affirmations

"Saying Affirmations daily is an excellent way to programme your mind to become positive in the future."

"I've heard of Affirmations. They are statements we repeat over and over again. Aren't they basically the same as Self Talk?" I asked.

I went on to explain how I'd attended positive thinking seminars in which we were exhorted to talk positively to ourselves, to say such things as "I can do it. I'm the best. I like myself. *I want to be a top ... ...* (whatever my field of work is)".

"That's the idea" said Peter. "It's a good way to improve your self esteem.

It is most important that you phrase your Affirmation in positive language, and that it is a statement of fact or belief - in a personal, positive, present tense form - as though the goal was already accomplished. And we suggest that you affirm the condition you want at least 25 times, once a day.

For example, if you were to say '*I want to be top in my field*' as you stated, or '*I will be top in my field*', the phrase '*I want to be*' can be countered by the fact that many people believe '*You don't get everything you want*'."

"When you say '*I will be*' you are talking about the future - and the mind works in the present. Until you believe you are capable and worthy of being top in your field, the mind will delay the end result.

It's important you use the correct words, such as 'I work as a person who is top in this field'; and then imagine yourself carrying out the necessary activities.

You also imagine how you would be, and feel, when you achieve the target. Then your mind will add it to your belief system as a 'fact', and your whole being will automatically work towards matching the reality of your belief system.

When we say Affirmations externally, we also say them internally. They affect the way we feel and the beliefs we have of ourself. That's why regularly repeated positive Affirmations have such a profound effect on our lives.

As you said, you realise that you are already making many positive and negative Affirmations every day in the form of Self Talk. Why not take control and make them positive, so they will work for you?

It is important to remember that deciding to make a change of habit, attitude, or personal situation, will not bring about that change."

"To make a change of any kind, the easiest way is to develop a goal, control your Self Talk, and use Affirmations which will change your Self Image.

So, establish a goal, and make a mental picture of what it will be like when the change has taken place.

Next, write your Affirmation."

"Can you provide me with some guide-lines for writing my Affirmations?" I asked.

"Yes" replied Peter. "Here is a set of notes from one of my courses which I'm sure will interest you. They cover the points necessary ... ..."

1. MAKE THEM PERSONAL

You can only make Affirmations regarding yourself. YOU are changing YOUR Self Image. Only you can control the input of Visualisation and Affirmations that brings about the change to your Self Image.

In most cases your Affirmation will be an "I" statement.

As with most guidelines, there are exceptions. If you, and your family or work group, agree on a joint goal, it is possible to write a "WE" Affirmation. For example, you and your family or work group set a joint goal. In this case you affirm both the "we" joint goal, and your individual part of reaching the goal.

2. MAKE THEM POSITIVE

Write your Affirmations in a positive sentence structure. You must vividly paint the picture of the change you want in a positive statement, for example, "I am energetic", "I have confidence".

3. KEEP THEM PRESENT TENSE

The reason you use the present tense for Affirmations is that this is the only time frame the Subconscious mind operates on.

4. INDICATE ACHIEVEMENT

Statements like "I am" and "I have" clearly express to the Subconscious the image of your behavioural change you want.

The more you subconsciously act AS IF you are already in possession of that quality or change, the faster your Self Image will make it occur in your life.

5. LOOK AT YOURSELF

Make the changes in your Self Image that you desire, affirm the qualities that are best for you.

Look at yourself, in relation to yourself alone, rather than in comparison with anyone else.

6. USE ACTION WORDS

Describe the activity you are affirming in terms that create an image of you performing in an easy and relaxed manner.

Statements starting with "I easily", "I quickly", "I enjoy", "I love to", "I thrive on" and "I show" carry an image of action and accomplishment which makes you feel neither threatened nor pushed.

7. INCLUDE EXCITEMENT WORDS

Put as much excitement as you can in the wording of your Affirmations by vividly affirming your behaviour in colourful terms. Write your Affirmations in a manner that creates fun, pride, happiness, accomplishment.

Some examples of starting phrases include "I happily", "I lovingly" and "I enthusiastically". These words help with the excitement of achieving your goals.

8. COVER NUMEROUS AREAS

Look at growth in many sections of your life, rather than one or two areas.

To ensure balance, ask yourself "Am I leaving out anything? Am I under-emphasising or over-emphasising the value of some parts of my life?"

9. CHOOSE ACHIEVABLE GOALS

Choose language that works for you, and set your sights on goals that match your personal life plan. Select goals worthy of your effort.

Be specific, and allow appropriate time frames. Avoid using absolutes such as "I always", "every time I" or "I'll never".

10. KEEP THEM TO YOURSELF

Your PERSONAL Affirmations are for you ONLY. Reveal your Affirmations to only those people who can help you attain your goals more quickly, as some people seem to enjoy reminding you of the "old Self Image".

"If you use these guides, your Affirmations will be effective.

The easiest way to write an Affirmation is to decide what you want to change.

Then get a clear picture in your mind of how you will act with the new habit, e.g. carrying out the job, enjoying the income.

Next, write a description of your picture in one sentence - and there is your Affirmation.

Be sure to put the description in your own words and style, as you would say it, so it sounds like you.

When you are satisfied with the wording of your Affirmations, transfer them to small systems cards so they will be easy to carry around with you. You may want to make several copies; one to carry, one for your desk at work, and another set for your bedside cupboard ... ..."

Here are some sample Affirmations that you can adapt for yourself.

1. I like and respect myself. I know I am a worthy, capable and valuable person.

2. I am optimistic about life, and I look forward to and enjoy new challenges to my awareness.

3. I show great concern for people's feelings.

4. I easily anticipate and experience events in my imagination before they actually occur.

5. I help my family members in any way I can.

6. I make people feel good about life and their place in the universe.

7. I have an excellent free flowing memory with clear and easy recall.

8. I am a true professional in my approach to my job activities.

9. I keep abreast of current information and can cope with any challenge that arises.

10. It's fun and easy to be organised.

* * * * * *

Today's Preparation

Determines

Tomorrow's

Achievements

Robert Todd

Using Affirmations

"What is the best procedure when using Affirmations?" I asked.

"Firstly, say your Affirmation several times each day" Peter replied. "There is nothing magic in saying the words other than to have a consistent trigger.

The best times to say or read, and imprint your Affirmations, are generally early in the morning and just before you go to sleep, or when you are carrying out associated tasks. Repetition of the Affirmation is essential.

Next, see your goal as you say your Affirmation. Vividly imagine and experience yourself clearly having accomplished the change you want, or the end result you intend to create.

Through this constructive imagery, you are replacing old Self Images with new pictures of how you want to feel and act.

Remember, you are practising and experiencing the change consciously to begin with - and through your picturing, you are turning your expectations over to the Subconscious. Very quickly you will begin moving easily and naturally to your new performance reality."

"Finally, feel the emotion you want. This is very important for impact.

Gather up the feelings you know will accompany the accomplished goal, and enjoy them each time you imprint your Affirmation. The Affirmation will affect your system in a positive way, in direct proportion to the frequency you use vividness and emotional involvement."

* * * * * * *

Law 6

WORDS CREATE OUR FUTURE

"We create our own future. We have control over our future. No-one else controls it.

We control it by the words, the phrases, the Self Talk, and expectations that we have. We can either make the future work positively for us, or we can create an unhappy, unsuccessful future, and no-one can stop us."

"What do you mean?"

"Your 'now' was your future, in the past. The restrictions you have on you now, were developed from your previous experiences and statements others made to you about these experiences.

As you proceeded through life, many of these were confirmed. For example, if you carried out some activity, and you decided or someone told you that you were hopeless, you probably developed a statement such as '*I am no good at ... ...* ' or '*I always have trouble with ... ...*'

These have become your present reality.

If you change the 'now', you change the future."

"Therefore, when you eliminate statements such as *'I always have trouble with ... ... '*, *'I have never been sure of ... ... '* *'I find it difficult to ... ... '* you remove the restricting beliefs based on your past experiences, the beliefs that stifle your present. Having removed these restrictions, you can enjoy the 'now' and look forward to a limitless future."

"So, for most of us, the future is dependent on what actually happened to us in the past?" I asked.

"Yes, Thomas. You see, we have beliefs about our capabilities, built-in boundaries on our future growth. We constantly reinforce these boundaries when we say *'I can't'*, *'I'm no good at it'*, *'I always get it wrong'*, *'With my luck I'll probably fail'*, *'It's impossible'*.

The barriers of today were created in the 'now' of the past. So, to create the future you would like, you will start using phrases that establish positive beliefs about yourself and your environment, in the now. This will propel you towards the future you want.

Use only positive language until it becomes a reality. By doing this, the present time will become your positive past, upon which your positive future will be built."

* * * * * * *

Words Create Our Future

"What are our capabilities?" I asked.

"Our abilities are far greater than many imagine" said Peter. "Unfortunately, for most people, their abilities are what they believe them to be.

There's a story which comes from the Olympic Games.

A Russian weight lifter was attempting to lift more than 600 pounds. No matter what his coach said, he was unable to get past this barrier.

One day the coach came in while the weight lifter was not there, and had a set of weights re-marked so they indicated slightly less.

When the weight lifter arrived the next day, the coach carried over the weights, putting them onto the bar, adding them up to 600 pounds. He said to his protege 'I'd like you to start with 3 lifts of 600 pounds. Take your time and we'll see how you're going today'.

The weight lifter stood there, lifted the 600 pounds, took a short rest, lifted the 600 again, took a short rest, and again lifted the 600. At the end of this exercise, the coach said 'That's fantastic. You've just lifted 620 pounds'!"

"The weight lifter couldn't believe it, so the coach told him how he had altered the markings. They rolled the weights over to the scales, the weight lifter placed them on - and realised that he had in fact broken the barrier.

He was convinced that he could lift 600 pounds, yet in reality he could lift more. The barrier was broken, and so he went on to win a gold medal in the Olympics.

The barriers were in the mind of the weight lifter.

To achieve this kind of result yourself, discipline is necessary. You have to overcome a lifetime of negative programmes, plus the continuing bombardment of negatives you hear every day.

It seems most people use only about 3 - 4% of the mind, and most of them can learn to develop their potential further.

You know that the words you use are shaping your life, therefore decide whether you want to go beyond your present limits, or remain the same. You have the choice to change your future, and this can be achieved by changing your language in the present."

* * * * * *

TODAY

IS THE

TOMORROW

YOU

WORRIED ABOUT

YESTERDAY

Robert Todd

The Secret Language

This framed saying hangs near the entrance to Peter's office:

By Choosing

Our Words

We Choose The Life

We Want To Live

Robert Todd

We Choose The Words We Use

As we stopped to contemplate those words, Peter said "The fact that we can choose our words gives us tremendous power.

It gives us control over ourselves, our destiny, our future, our relationships, our job, our environ-ment, the lot.

We can choose to be in a positive environment, where we see success, where we achieve; or we can choose to see negatives, failure.

The fact that we choose our words is powerful. We can choose our words, internally and externally. We can use Self Talk in a positive way or a negative way. It's up to us.

Positive words and statements move us towards our goals. Negative words and statements move us away from our goals.

We 'make' ourselves or 'destroy' ourselves. We can influence others, positively or negatively.

We can choose words that will attract people who will be beneficial to us, or we can attract people who will activate negative situations.

No-one tells us what to say. We have the choice."

I Believe That Whatever

Our Current Situation Is,

We Can Alter It If We Want To,

By Making A Conscious

Decision To Do So,

And

By Changing Our Language .

We Can Re-Write Our

Psychological Script

Using The Laws Of

Positive Language .

Robert Todd

"What you're suggesting again, Peter, is to choose carefully every word we use?"

"What I'm suggesting is that people start listening to what they're saying, so they can remove any words that create demotivation in themself or the people around them, which could diminish future potential.

They can choose words that are progressive, inspiring them, enhancing them, giving them creative ideas, words that open their minds to unlimited expectations and goals."

I thought over what Peter had said about choosing the words we use, and realised I had been using a lot of negative words and statements. When I started to replace negative words with positive ones, I felt much happier within myself.

Already I can clearly identify the negativity around me and take action to avoid being infected. In fact, I find myself wondering why others are so negative, until I see the "old me" in them.

It seems as though negative people do not believe they think and talk negatively. They say they are being realistic. They are able to give you a hundred reasons why something won't work, and no reasons why it will. They logic it out to justify themselves.

It's amazing the number of people I now notice who put themselves down on a regular basis. It's as though they are programmed to look on the gloomy side of life.

For many people, the subconscious is a vast repository of negative experiences and reactions, mainly as a result of the environment in which they live. They harbour feelings of guilt or inadequacy;

and feelings of fear for their future. These fears are strengthened by the everyday expressions from people they meet.

There is a constant stream of bad news in newspapers, on TV and radio - people drowning, hundreds killed in a plane crash, protestors shot down in cold blood, the 85 year old woman who had her walking stick kicked away and was robbed as she fell to the ground, rape, murder, cruelty, and the constant complaints about inflation, the high cost of living, unemployment. It goes on and on.

If we control what we read, listen to, and talk about, we can go a long way towards controlling our personal environment.

Many of the commercials we see on TV, for example, are negative. Some teach us to be doubtful, or highlight our poor complexion or poor health, tell us we are over-weight, and make us feel apprehensive about our relationships, our safety, and our future.

Some commercials actually promote sickness. Many teach us that telling lies is O.K.

The soapies on TV concentrate on the negative aspects of life. They are full of suicides, divorces, incestuous relationships, runaway kids, alcoholics, gang wars, and work dodgers.

So, with your eyes and ears being bombarded with this material, and people saying "not bad" instead of "good", and openly denigrating themselves, it's quite a challenge to be positive.

Is this the reason my positive attitude had not been as effective as I'd planned?

I thought back to how negativity had appeared like a virus in my organisation.

When I started my business, it was only my wife and I working from home. After a while we employed a couple of people and moved into a commercial building. We were a tight-knit, happy, positive group.

Our little group was able to maintain a positive environment because, during the establishment period, all of us were fired-up by our enthusiasm and early success, and we were able to ward off the negative "virus".

When the initial enthusiasm waned, and new people joined us, then the negative virus started to move in.

The "virus" of negativity seems common in our society, and I now recognise that negative language is contagious, and how it permeated our company.

"The wonderful thing" Peter continued "is that once you are aware that you have a choice, and you know the power of positive language, you can create a positive environment for yourself and those around you, by choosing the words you utter.

Your family can become positive, by eliminating negative words and phrases. By guiding your staff to use positive language, you can create a positive environment in your workplace."

"I suppose" I said "if we carried that idea to its widest point, then the whole world could become a positive environment?"

"Yes" said Peter. "And to achieve a positive environment means that each person would change."

"O.K." I said. "I will start with myself, then help my family, my friends, and those at work."

As A Human Being,

You Are Free To Will

Whatever State Of Being

You Desire,

Through The Use Of Your

Thoughts And Words .

There Is A Great Power There .

It Can Be A Blessing

Or A Curse .

It Is Entirely Up To You .

Sir Lawrence Olivier

"Can you give me a programme to follow that will allow me to use positive language to create for myself, and others around me, a positive environment?"

"As you know" replied Peter "positive language requires constant awareness of the words and phrases you are using, a culling of the negatives, and a habit of carefully selecting positive words and phrases."

"What are the steps, Peter?"

* * * * * * *

Steps To Positive Language

The steps taken to become positive are:

1. Become aware of the language you are currently using.

2. Decide that you want to change.

3. Become aware of the individual words, for example 'try, but, should', and work on replacing these.

4. Become aware of your Self Talk. As you notice any negative Self Talk, immediately develop a positive statement to replace it.

5. Become aware of the statements you make. Begin to modify language. Substitute positive phrases for negative ones.

6. Allow language to guide you into a more positive world. Be relaxed about it.

"As you follow that programme" Peter said "you will find yourself becoming more positive, more successful and content each day, without effort on your behalf. Your new positive language will automatically direct you into a more positive world.

It will be a challenge for you to use positive language. Stick with it, Thomas. You will find that by being aware of the words you use, and by gradually introducing positive words and phrases into your language, good things will start to happen for you."

"They have already" I said. "Thanks for the advice you've given me."

During the weeks I had been meeting with Peter and adjusting my language, I had noticed a change in my attitude, and in the attitude of others toward me. A whole new world is open to me.

In observing my vocabulary, I found I used the word "difficult" a lot. I began changing my language by concentrating on eliminating a word a week. The first week, it was "difficult", then "try", then "but".

We have a money box at home into which I dropped 20 cents every time I used the "negative word for the week". A friend of mine asks his business associates to give him a gentle punch when he uses any negative word.

I've been at it for quite a while now, and still slip into some negative words and phrases. Being aware of the fact that I've slipped is important, and I recall the word mentally each time and change it.

Positive language has really worked for me. Its power can be understood only when you put it into practice.

When you become aware of your scripts, spend some time analysing your language and the attitudes you've adopted over the years; when you know what's in your script, and realise you have the freedom to change it; then a new life begins.

KNOW THYSELF

These two words were written above the Temple of Apollo at Delphi, which was built in the year 320 B.C, and philosophers for centuries have continued to exhort us to know ourselves.

Assuming you want to change - that's a personal decision. People usually want to change because they want to be happier and more successful.

People Change

When They Realise

They Can Change

The Secret Language

IT'S UP TO YOU.

$$[0\backslash0]$$

I pray, as you move through this earthly plane, that you will understand the power of the word.

Quotations From This Book

There are two kinds of knowledge, knowledge we know and knowledge we can find.

Anonymous

The individual's whole experience is built upon the plans of his language.

Henry Delacroix

Men imagine that their minds have command of language, yet language bears rule over their mind.

Francis Bacon

Change our words, change our way of speaking, change our way of thinking, then we can change other aspects of our life.

Robert Todd

Change your language and you change your thoughts.

Robert Todd

Change your thoughts and you change your world.

> Norman Vincent Peale

When you understand the Laws of Positive Language, when you use positive language, when you experience the power of positive language, you can have positivity working for you.

Language is a tool that extends beyond expressing our wants and feelings clearly. It knows the effect our words have, the reactions they create, in our own minds and in the minds of others.

> Robert Todd

Through positive language, we can change our world.

> Robert Todd

Look at her, a prisoner of the gutter, condemned by every syllable she utters.

> George Bernard Shaw

The words we use have a magical effect on us as we use them.

> Aldous Huxley

If you say it, you think it. When you eliminate it from your verbal vocabulary, you eliminate it from your thinking vocabulary.

> Robert Todd

The secret of being positive is to keep your attention on all subjects positively and express them in positive language.

> Robert Todd

Do not let what you cannot do, interfere with what you can do.

> John Wooden

By choosing the appropriate words, it is possible to transform the mind of an individual.

> Anonymous

Unless you consciously feed your mind with positive statements, others will fill it with negative ones.

> Robert Todd

Every time you say positive words, you simultaneously visualise positive scenes and experience positive feelings. That is why it's important to use positive language at all times.

> Robert Todd

I choose to be healthy and free. All is well in my world.

> Louise L. Hay

Every day in every day I'm getting better and better.

> Emil Coue

People speak confidently because they are successful, and people are successful because they speak confidently.

Anonymous

Positive language is the key to positive thinking. Belief is the power that turns the key.

Robert Todd

Whatever you can do or dream you can, begin it. Boldness has genius, magic and power in it. Begin it now.

Johann Wolfgang Goethe

To be positive outside, be positive inside.

Robert Todd

Today's preparation determines tomorrow's achievements.

Today is the tomorrow that you worried about yesterday.

Anonymous

By choosing our words, we choose the life we want to live.

I believe that whatever our current situation is, we can alter it if we want to, by making a conscious decision to do so, and by changing our language. We can re-write our psychological script using the Laws of Positive Language.

Robert Todd

As a human being, you are free to will whatever state of being you desire through the use of your thoughts and words. There is great power there. It can be a blessing or a curse. It is entirely up to you.

Sir Lawrence Olivier

People change when they realise they can change.

Anonymous

* * * * * * *

LISTING OF NEGATIVE INDICATORS

Quick reference to locate Negative Indicators, which are in italics in this book. If you make any of these statements, this book will help you improve your life, and become more successful and positive.

THE SEARCH (page 1)

> There are no shortcuts to success
> Difficulty
> If I'm ever going to make it
> Bad luck comes in threes
> If at first you don't succeed, then try, try again
> Failure is but opportunity in disguise
> Try
> I wanted to succeed, but the rest of the world didn't want it
> But it isn't easy
> I hoped
> Problems
> Something that comes easily is not worth having
> But
> Win some - lose some
> If only

Tried
Impossible
I wish
If only I could
I ought to be able
But what do I do
Two heads are better than one
Maybe

THE APPROACH page 6)

But
Too good to be true
Problems

LESSON ONE (page 8)

Problem
I try to succeed, but it seems as if the world doesn't want it
I guess I am successful, but
I'm hoping to try and find out
I should be achieving them
I think
If it's possible
Maybe, there's a possibility that, if we tried, we might be successful
Win some, lose some
Bad luck comes in threes
Too good to be true

RIVERS OF REACTION (page 12)

I try to succeed, but it seems as if the world doesn't

want it
I'll try
Try to win, but don't get your hopes up
Tried
That's a good idea but
What you're saying is O.K. but
I should clear up my desk
Problem

POSITIVE THESAURUS (page 17)

Try
But
However
Should
Ought
Wish or Hope
If only
Impossible
Difficult
Problem
Just
Only

COMBINED NEGATIVES (page 21)

Don't think of an orange
Don't worry
Don't forget
No injuries
Don't forget to phone
Don't leave the machine running
Don't be late
Don't speed

Not wrong
Not difficult
No worries
No problems

DOUBLE NEGATIVES (page 27)

They're not an unattractive person
You're not wrong
We can't fail
That's not a bad idea

POSITIVE ENVIRONMENTS (page 31)

I can't solve the problem

SELF AND POSITIVE LANGUAGE (page 48)

Hopeless
A fool
I'm a dreadful cook
I haven't got much colour sense
Who would have me in their team
I'm a lousy letter writer
My memory is getting worse
Why does it always happen to me
I'm no good in the morning until I have a cup of coffee
I was out late last night, so I won't have any energy today
When I have to use the computer, I get confused
When I have a lot of homework, I get headaches
Anything I eat goes to fat
No matter what I eat, I put on weight
At this point in time
To tell you the truth

I'm being honest about this
Frankly speaking
I'm not sure
I'm not certain about that
With all due respect
Succeed or fail

CHILDREN AND POSITIVE LANGUAGE (page 57)

It's a mess
You can't paint
You're hopeless
See, he couldn't even keep in the lines
Have you ever seen a green man
What on earth have you done, you stupid child
You're a naughty, bad, or stupid, boy or girl
I can't do it
Wrong - mistake
You can't do that while I am cooking
Win - lose

PROVERBS AND TRUISMS (page 68)

It's too good to be true
I have no right to have it so good
It can't last
You must have the bad to appreciate the good
Win some, lose some
I told you so
Time is money
Don't be late, or you'll miss the boat
Look before you leap
Fools rush in where angels fear to tread
He who hesitates is lost

Robert Todd

    A stitch in time saves nine
    Money is the root of all evil
    Money doesn't grow on trees
    Honest people are poor
    Poor people are happy
    Something that comes easily is not worth having
    You can't be a millionaire without hard work
    Bad luck comes in threes
    The early bird catches the worm
    First in, best dressed
    There is the quick or the dead
    You can't count your chickens by breaking eggs
    Patience is a virtue, possess it if you can
    You can't win them all
    When all else fails, read the instructions
    If you don't know now, you never will
    There are no short cuts to success
    Two heads are better than one
    You can't get there from here
    No pain, no gain
    Wear clean underwear in case you get hit by a bus
    The good old days
    I was better off when

HEALTH (page 79)

    Take it easy; don't strain yourself
    You don't want heart problems like your father
    It was the strain and stress of the job that killed your father
    I seem unable to cope these days
    Everything is getting on top of me
    I seem to be depressed all the time
    Everything irritates me

The Secret Language

> I seem to be having more illness
> He makes me sick
> It makes me ill when I think of it
> I'll never survive without
> I'm dying to get there
> If you eat that, you'll be sick
> If you go outside without a jumper, you'll get a cold
> When there's a change in the weather, I get a cold
> If there are colds going around the office, I'm sure to get one
> I have been sitting next to someone who has a cole, so I will get one, for sure
> Air conditioners always affect me
> The person behind keeps coughing on me and I'm likely to get a cold
> I never get sick

SELF TALK (page 86)

> I hope it doesn't hurt too much
> I hate dentists
> I wonder if the dentist will find any holes
> That's like me
> That's unusual for me
> It's just a fluke
> I am; I'm not. I am; I'm not. I am; I'm not
> I have difficulty getting up in the morning
> I'm always late
> I sleep in and I don't hear the alarm clock

IMAGINATION AND BELIEF (page 92)

> We are only fooling ourselves if we think talking positively and expecting good things to happen can

actually make them happen
By substituting 'I'm a kind, loving person' for 'I'm a bad person whom no one likes' and expecting to change some of our character, is ridiculous
I guess I look at things in a negative way, but I can't change my personality
I believe your philosophy intellectually, but not emotionally
The words you use in positive language describe a situation unrealistically
Why can't I say 'I want to earn $500,000 a year' and have it come true
Why can't I jump from a 10 storey building after saying to myself 'I'll land safely on the ground'

AFFIRMATIONS (page 104)

> I want to be top in my field
> I will be top in my field
> You don't get everything you want

LAW 6 (page 114)

> I am no good at
> I always have trouble with
> I have never been sure of
> I find it difficult to
> I can't
> I'm no good at it
> I always get it wrong
> With my luck I'll probably fail
> It's impossible
>
> * * * * * * *

www.ingramcontent.com/pod-product-compliance
Lightning Source LLC
LaVergne TN
LVHW011710060526
838200LV00051B/2837